The Crow and the Daylight

Written by Frances Lee
Illustrated by Chantal Stewart

sundance

Contents

Preface

The Crow and the Daylight is based on a Native American myth.

Some myths try to explain a fact of nature, such as how the sun came to be in the sky.

3

A World of Darkness

Once upon a time, when the world was new, daylight was rare.

Only one village had daylight. The chief of that village guarded it very carefully and would not share it with other people.

All of the other villages had no daylight.

The people who lived in these villages
lived in darkness all of the time.
While some people slept, others worked.
The only light they had came
from their small oil lamps.

The people who lived in darkness
knew about the village
that had daylight.
They had tried and tried
to get it, but they
always failed.

7

One chief, however, was determined to capture
the daylight. He sent many young men
to find it, but they were never seen again.

The chief called his people together.
He offered a reward to the person
who was brave enough to bring the light
to their village. When the brave one returned,
he or she would be a chief.

At this meeting was a brave crow.
When Crow offered to find the
daylight, everyone laughed.

How could a crow get the
daylight when many men,
much stronger and braver
than Crow, had failed?

But Crow had made up his mind.

9

Crow Looks for Daylight

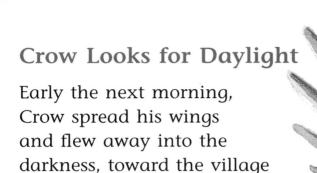

Early the next morning,
Crow spread his wings
and flew away into the
darkness, toward the village
that had daylight.

Crow flew on and on until his
wings grew very tired. But he
never stopped.

Crow flew for many days.
At last he could see light in the distance.
Soon the whole village came into view.
It was bathed in bright light.

The chief's dwelling was
in the center of the village.
Crow was sure that he would
find daylight inside there.

Crow hopped to the entrance of the chief's dwelling and looked inside. He could see the chief's granddaughter. The child was sitting on a warm fur rug, playing with toys.

Crow could also see a small, beautiful wooden box that glowed with light. He knew that the box was where the chief kept the daylight.

So Crow thought of a plan.

Crow quietly whispered a magic spell.

"Ya-ka-ty, ta-ka-ty, na-ka-ty-o.
Make me like a speck of dust.
No one will see me then, I trust."

At once Crow became no larger
than a tiny speck of dust. He floated into
the chief's dwelling, up to the child, and into
her hair. The child began to cry. The chief
asked her, "What is the matter, little one?"

"Ask to play with the box of
daylight," Crow whispered into
the child's ear.

And so the child asked the chief
for the box of daylight to
play with.

The box of daylight was the chief's most precious possession. But the child continued to cry and cry. And so he made sure that the box was locked and gave it to her.

"Go outside with the box of light," whispered Crow. The child walked to the entrance. Quick as a flash, Crow floated out of the child's hair.

"Ya-ka-ty, ta-ka-ty, na-ka-ty-o.
I don't want to be small.
I want to grow."

Suddenly, Crow was big again.
He grabbed the box in his beak
and flew away as fast as he could.

Crow Returns to the Village

Crow flew for many days. He flew on and on until his wings grew very tired. But he never stopped. At last, Crow arrived at his village.

It was very dark. Then he put down the beautiful wooden box.

"I have brought you daylight," said Crow, and he opened the box.

Instantly, the sun shone in the sky, and the whole land was filled with light. The people and the chief were so happy that they danced and sang. Then they made a feast in Crow's honor.

The people of the northern lands
have been grateful to Crow ever since.